Bride's Journal

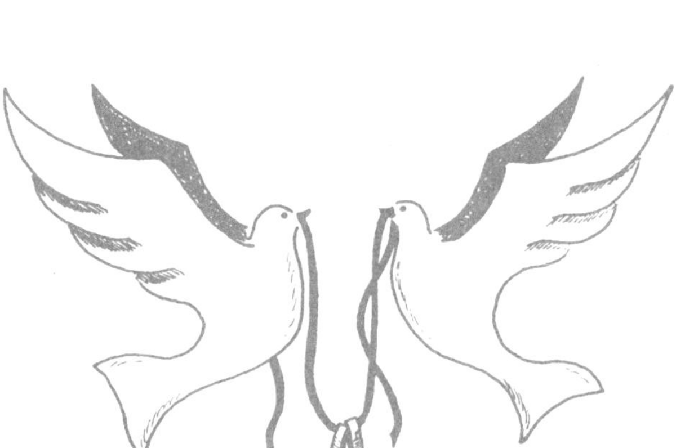

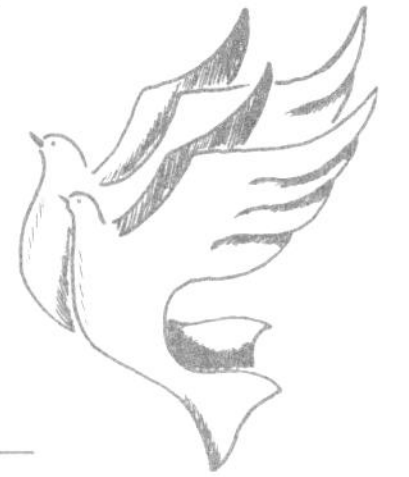

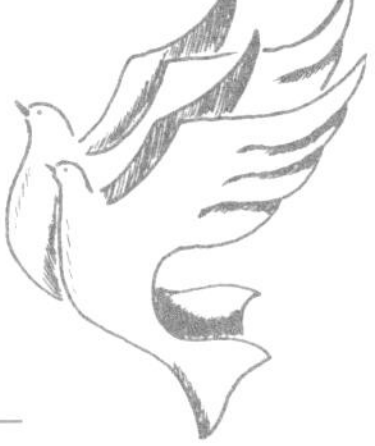

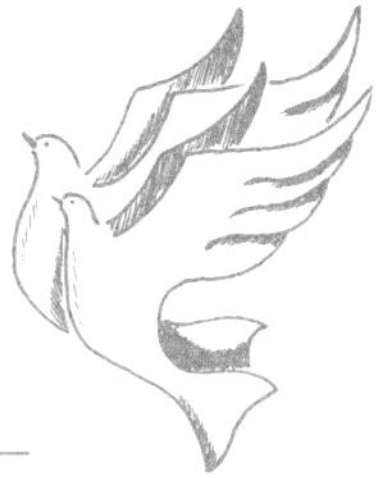

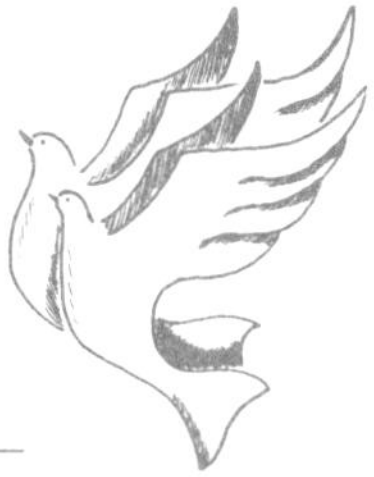

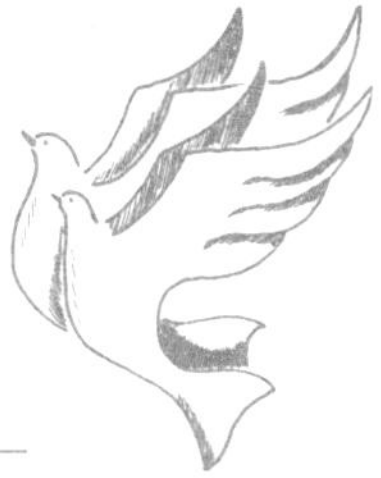

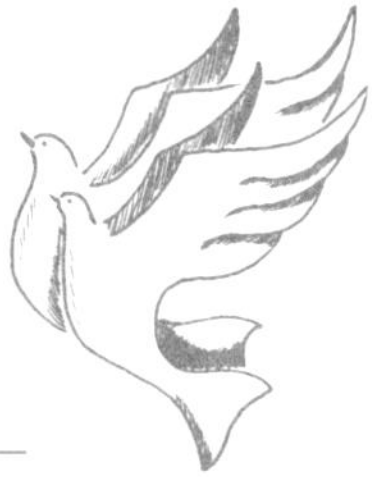

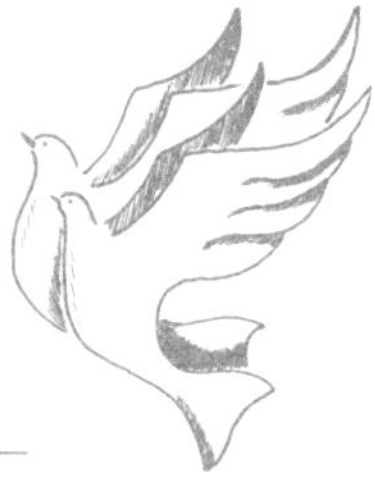

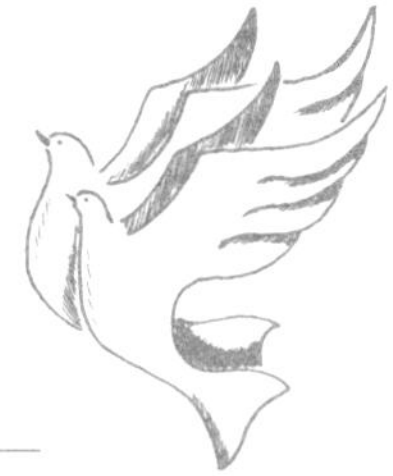

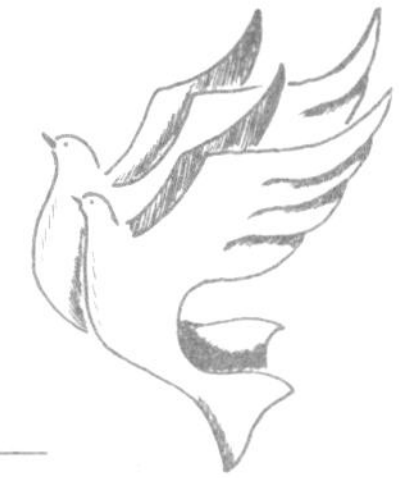

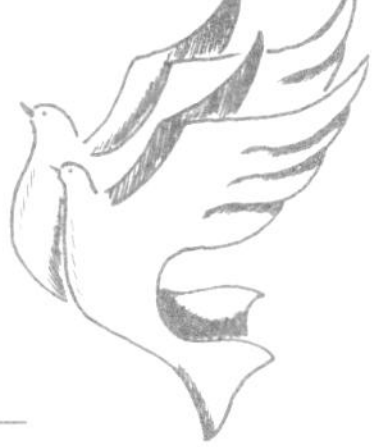

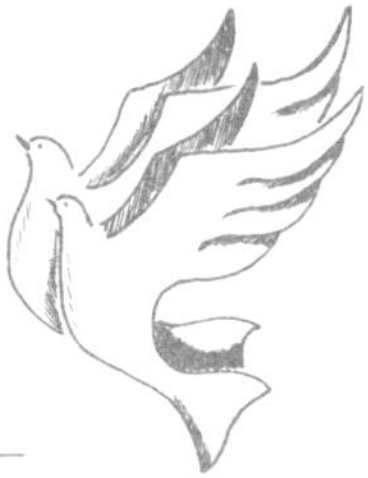

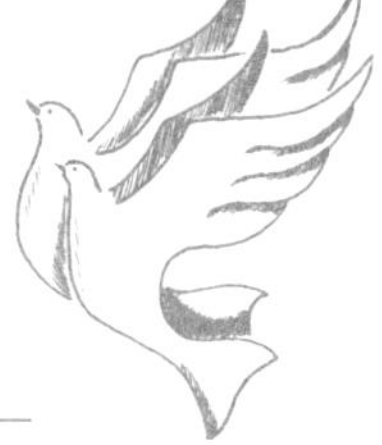

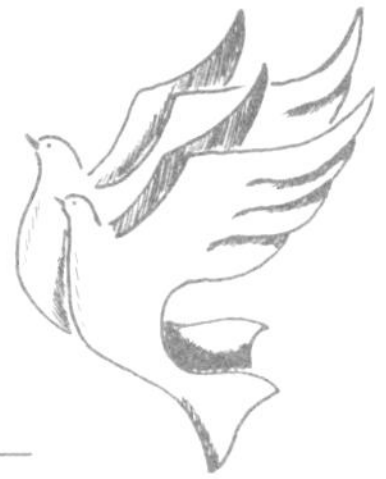

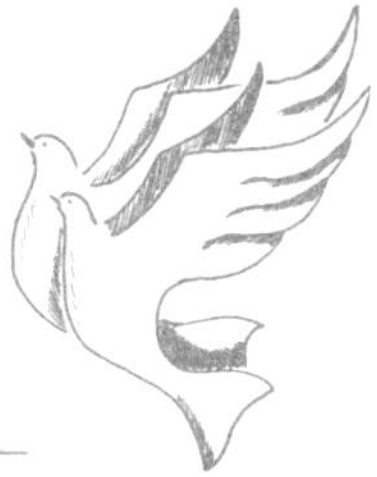

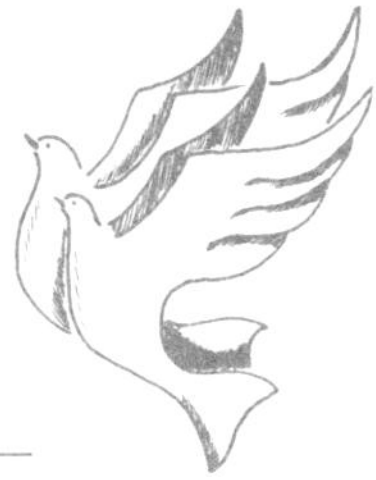

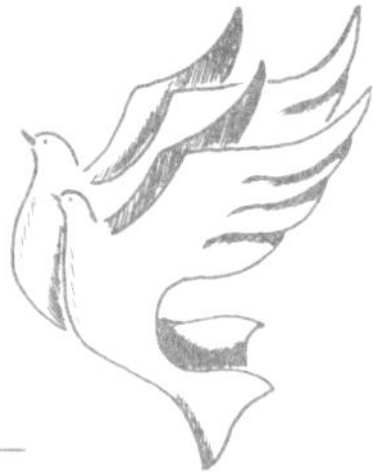

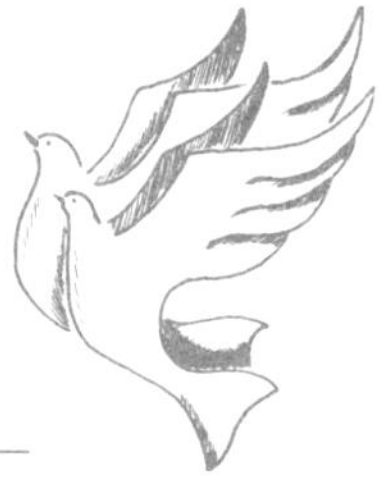

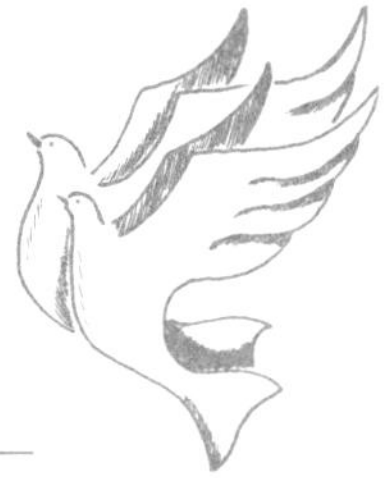

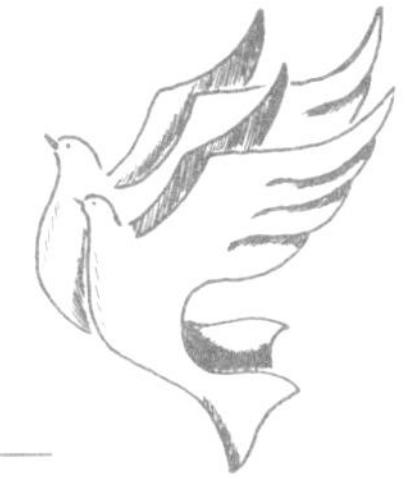

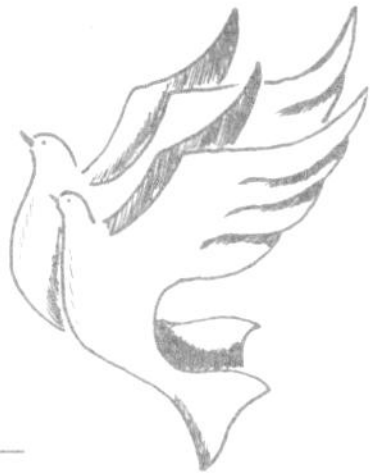

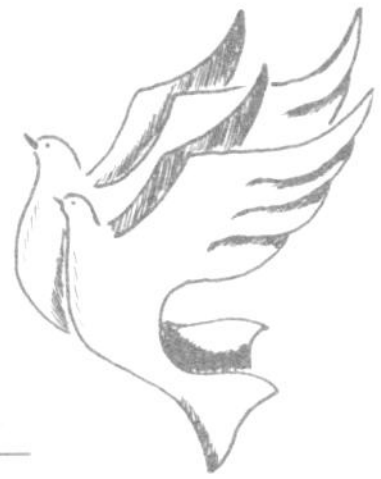

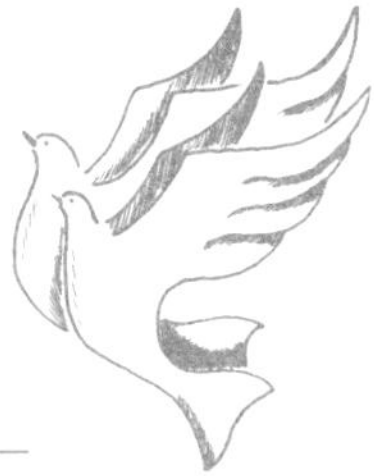

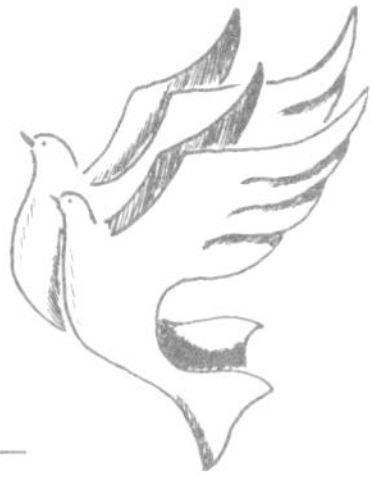

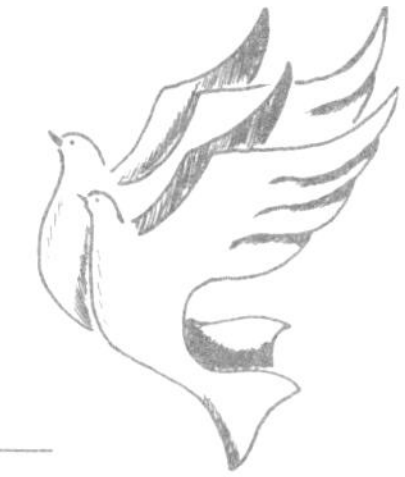

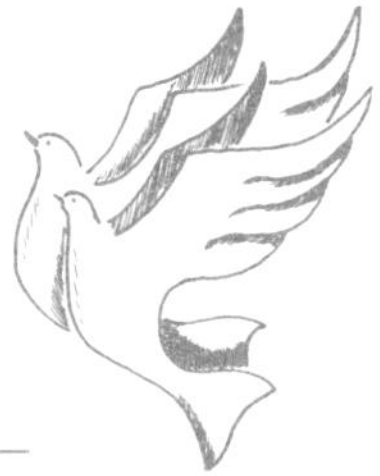

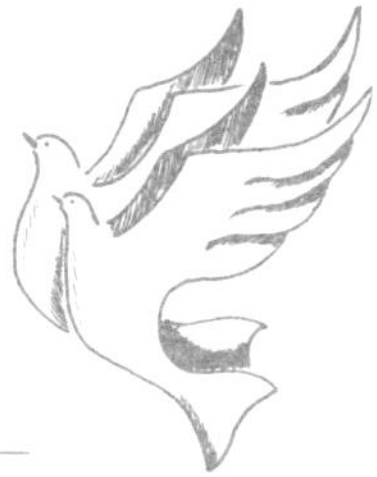

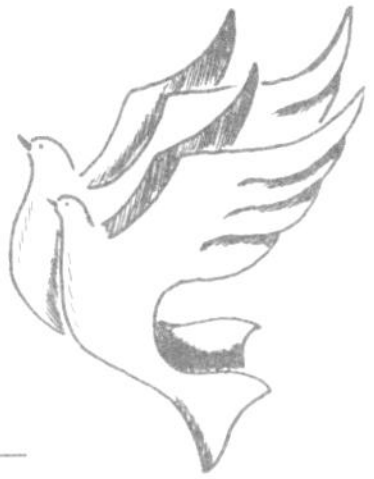

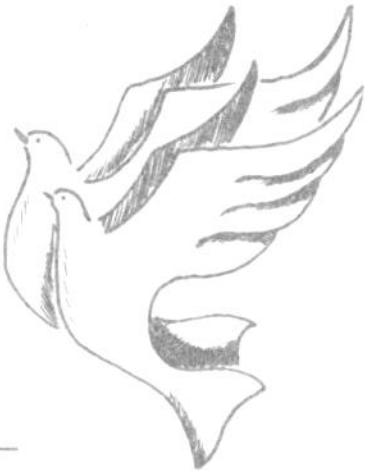

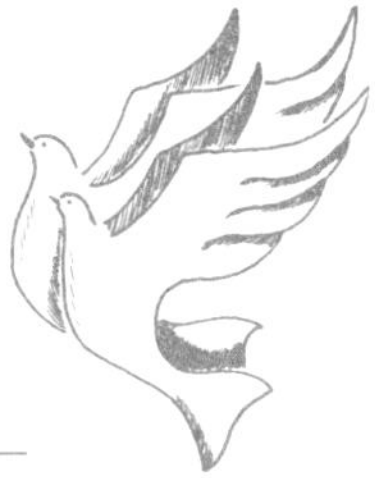

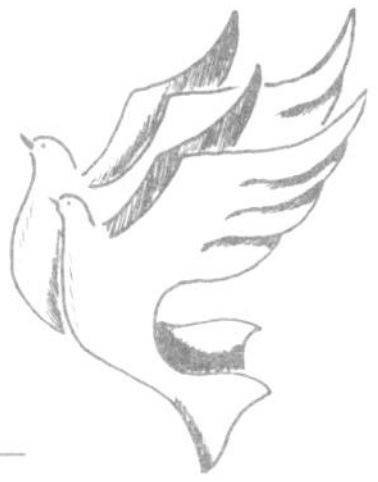

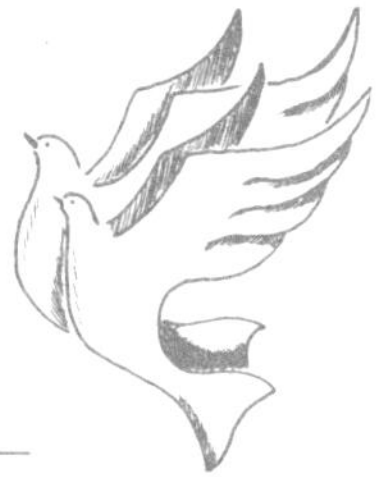

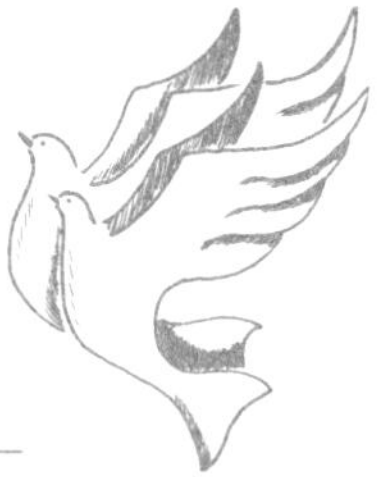

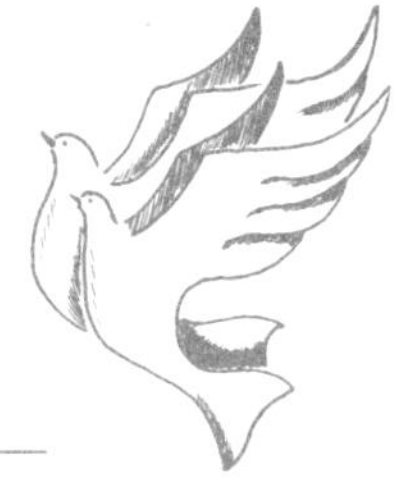

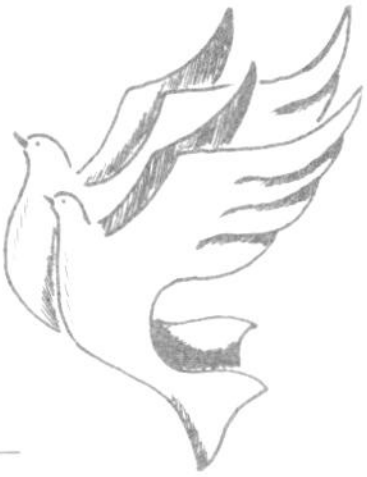

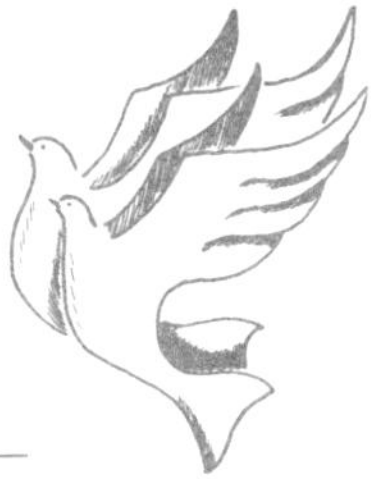

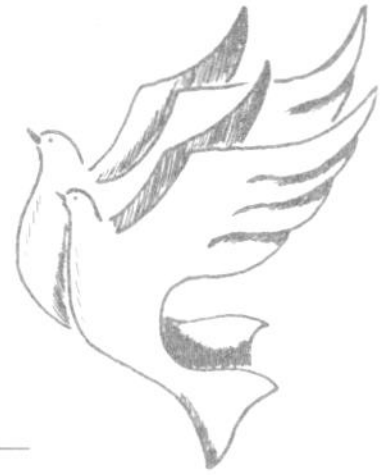

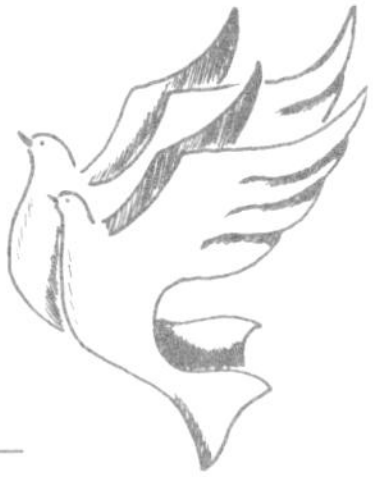

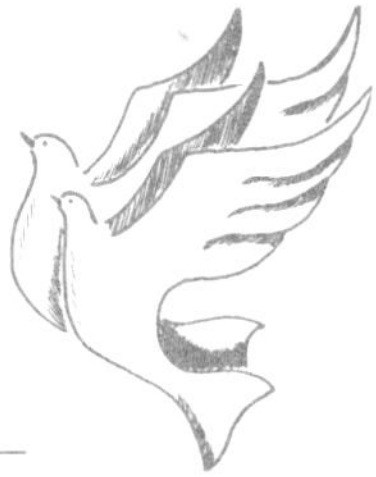

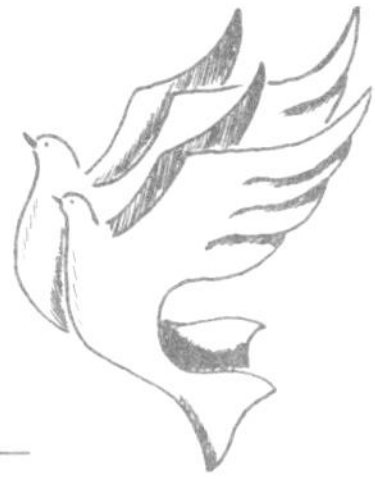

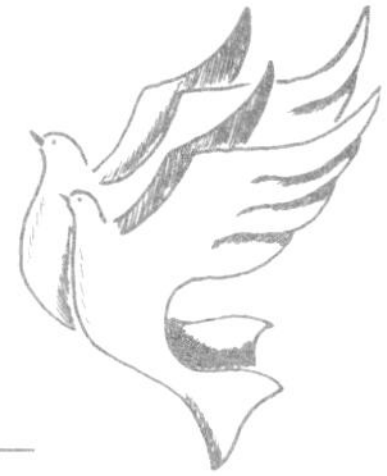

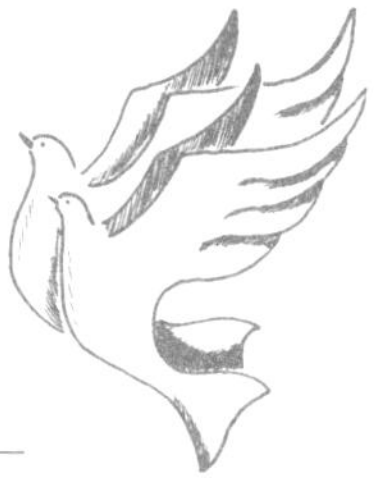

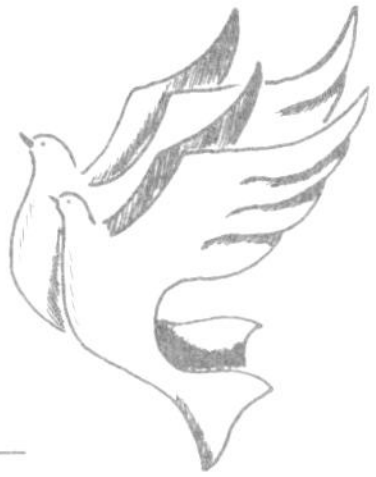

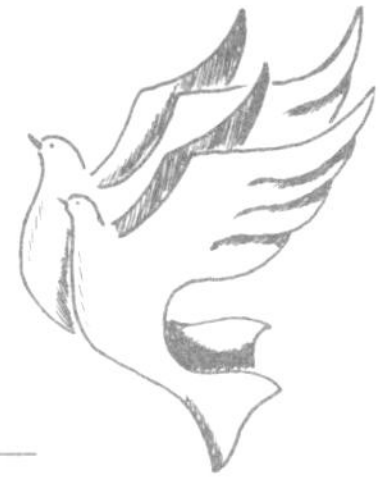

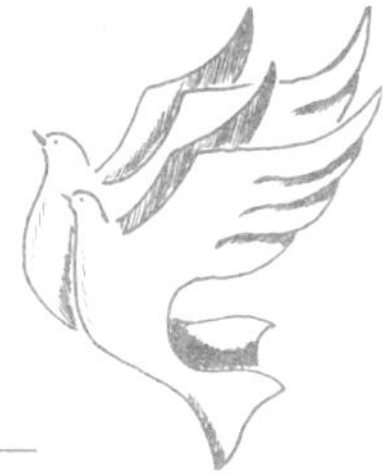

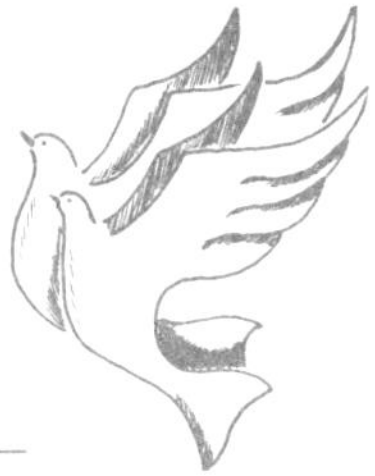

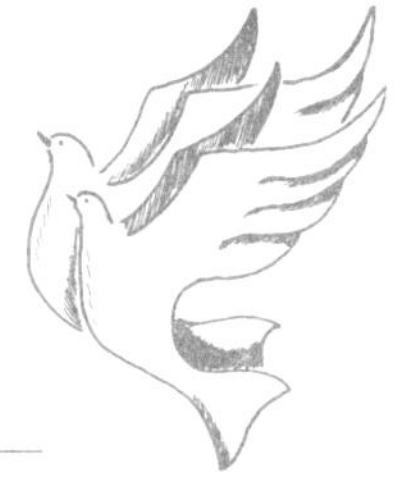

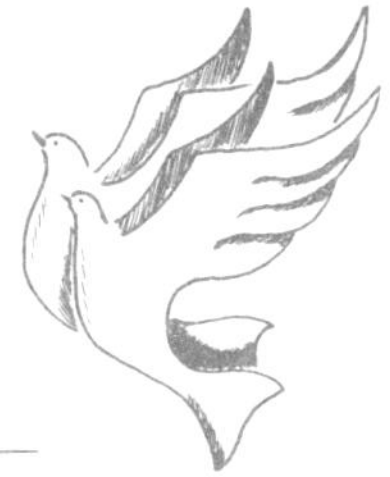

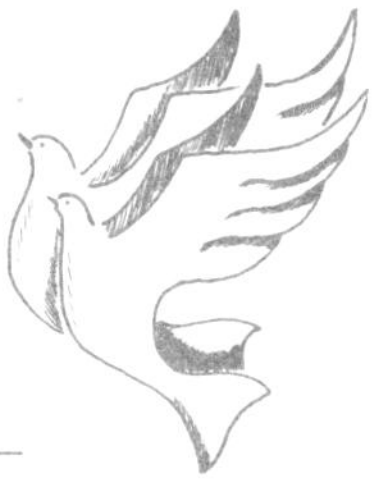

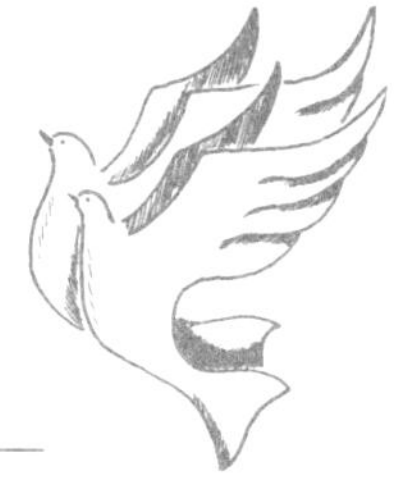

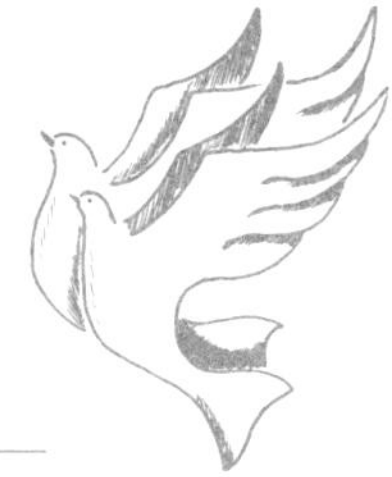

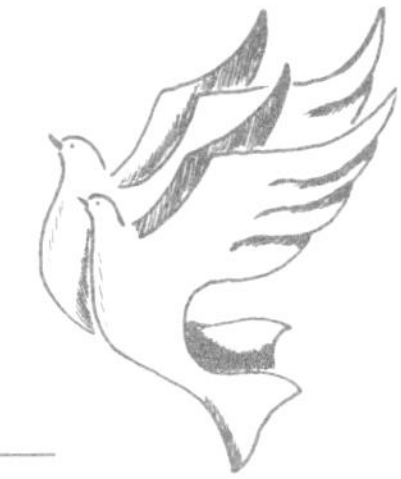

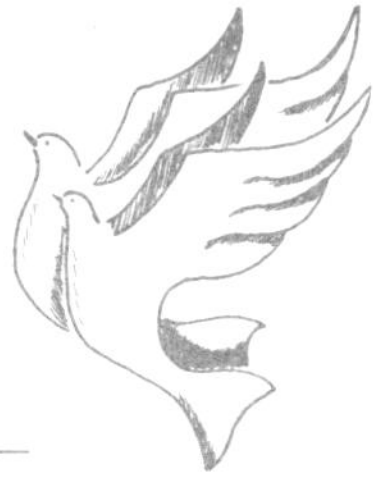

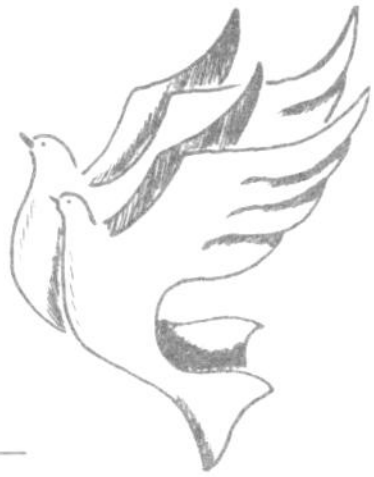

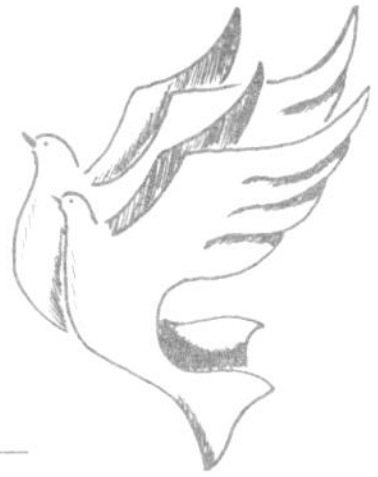

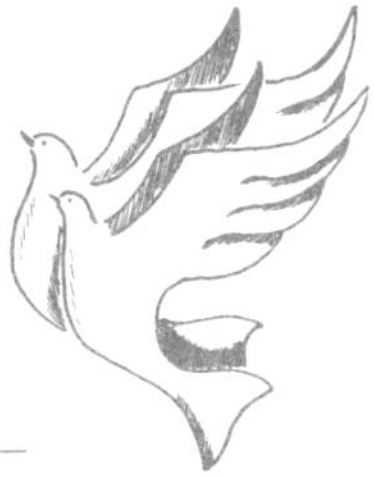

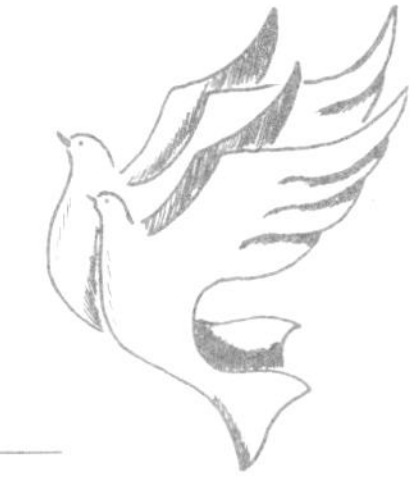

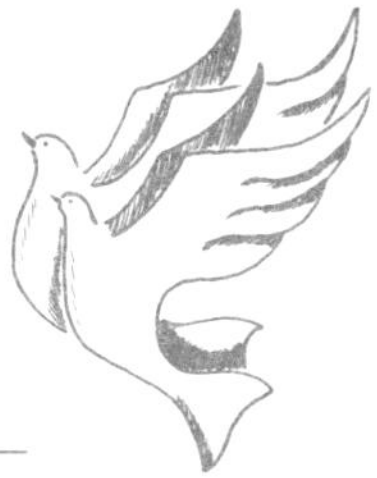

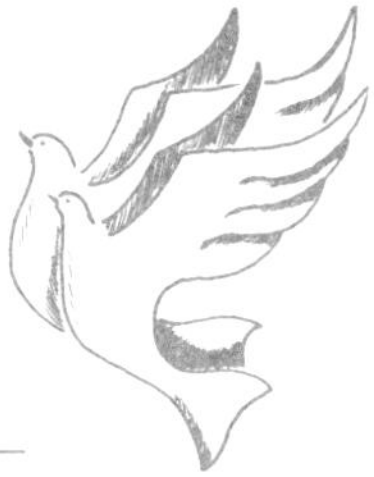

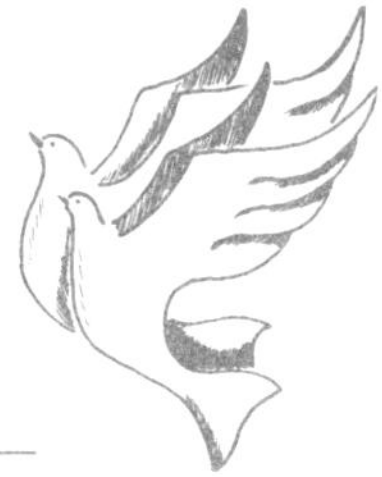

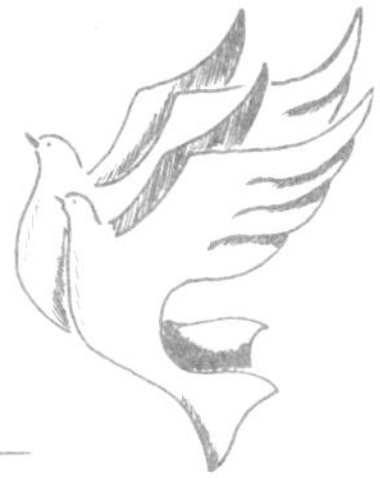

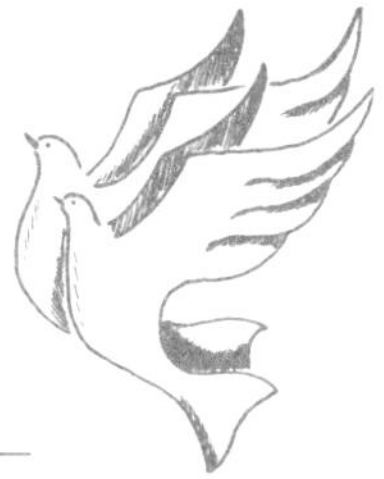

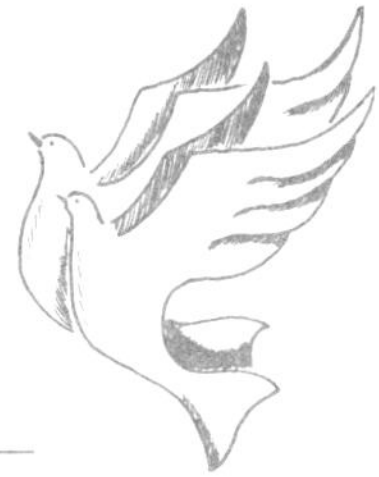

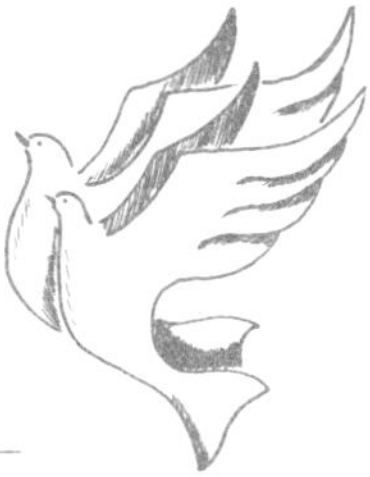

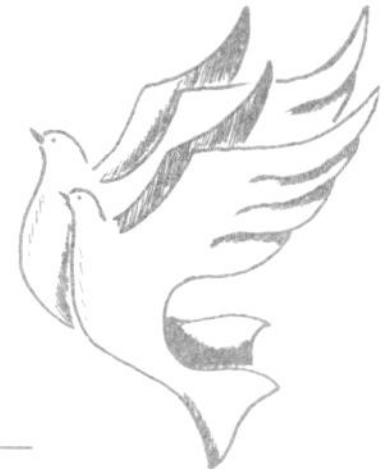

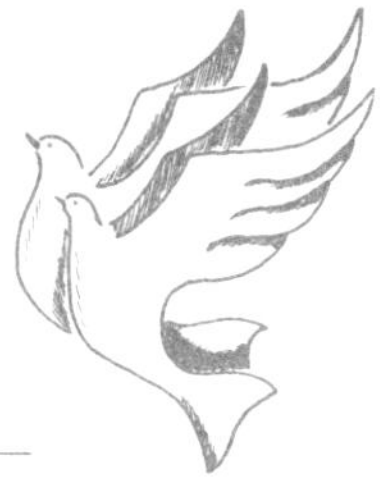

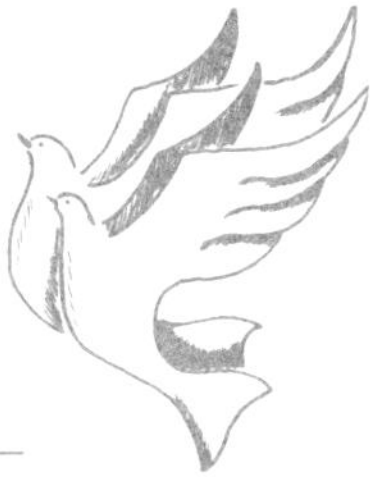

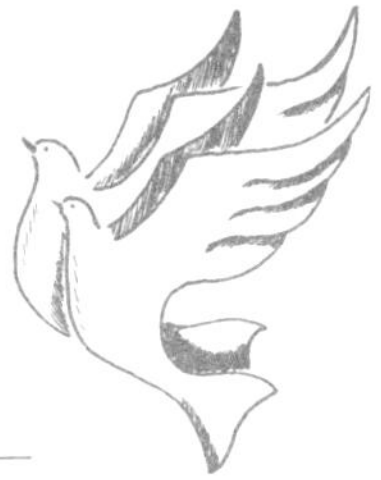

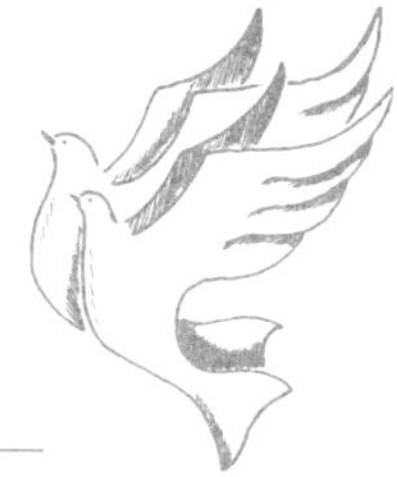

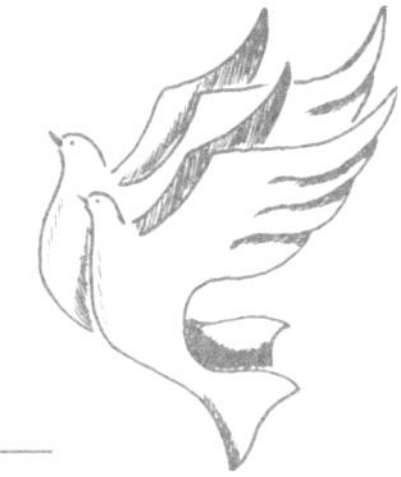

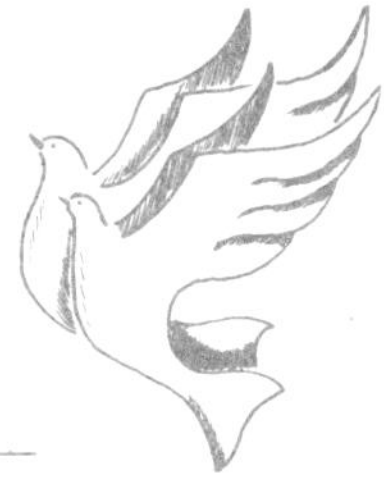

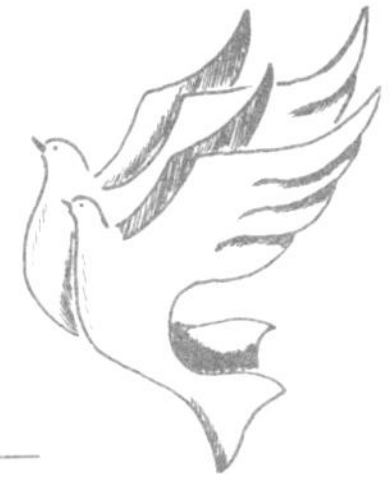

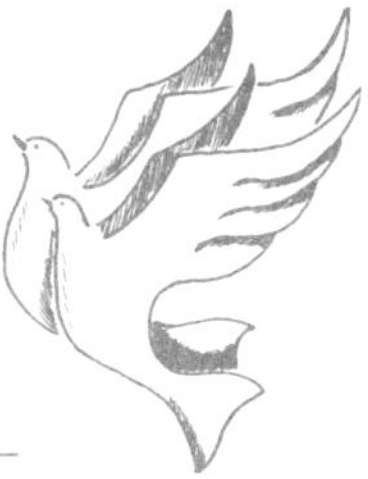

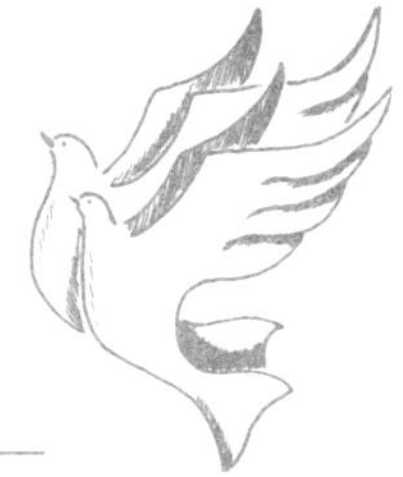

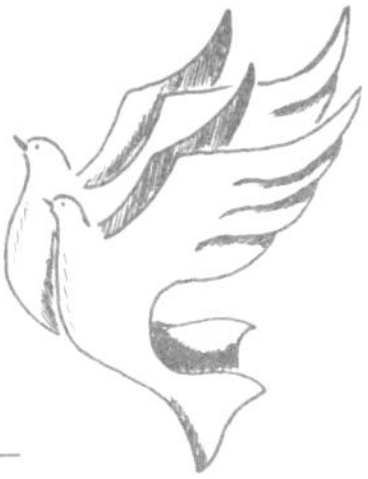

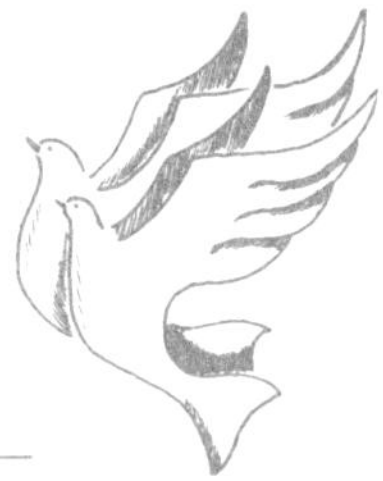

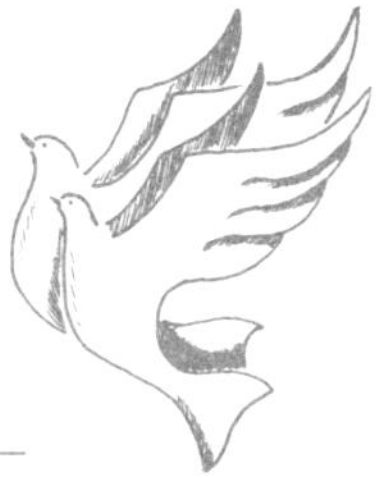

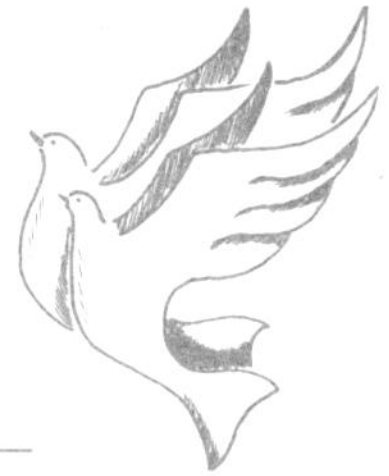

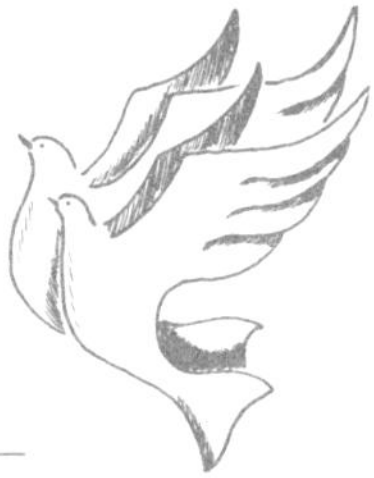

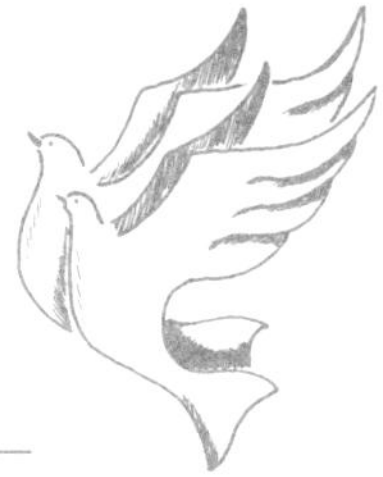

Designed by Janet Anastasio
Printed in Singapore
Cover Photograph by H. Armstrong Roberts
Illustrations by Shannon McNeely